I0416039

City of the Living Dead

(Fletcher Pratt & Laurence Manning)

Kartindo Books (Kartindo.com)

Contents

Kartindo Books (Kartindo.com)

Chapter I

THE sun sank slowly behind the far-off, torn and rocky crags, throwing up a last red glare like a shout of defiance as the white tooth of Herjehogmen mountain blotted the last beams from Alvrosdale. A deep-toned copper bell rang across the evening, and the young men and girls, leaving their dancing on the ice, came trooping up the path in little groups to the Hall of Assembly, laughing and talking. Their gay-colored clothes stood out brilliantly against the white background of the snow in the Northern twilight that often seems like day.

At the door of the Hall they parted-not without sadness, since for many it was the last parting-some going into the Hall, others passing on up the path to the line of houses. Those who entered were grave, though they had smiled not long before. Yet they were a goodly company for all that, some three-score in number and all in the fire of youth.

Within the hall might be seen benches; a great fire against one wall, and against the other the mouldering remains of those Machines that were the last relics of the days of old. At the center was a dais with places for the elders of Alvros, and midmost among these sat a man full of years, but in no wise feeble. Strong, stern, white-headed, he bore on one arm the silver band of authority, and in his hand he held a small, shiny Machine, round in shape and with a whiteface which bore twelve characters written in black. As the youth took their places, he twisted this Machine, so that it rang a bell, loud and stridently. Then there was silence, and the old man rose to speak.

"My friends," said he, "you will leave Alvrosdale tomorrow. Your skis are even now prepared; your glider wings await you outside. In this Hall of Assembly, which was once the House of Power, we are met tonight, as is the custom of our people, that I may tell the story of the last of the Anglesk and warn you of the dangers you will meet. Some of you-God grant it may be few!-will be caught in treacherous winds and flung against the Mountain of the South to die.

Some may be caught by the Demon Power, whom the Anglesk worshipped. Some will find green fields and prosperity, and will meet the others of our folk who have gone before . . . But a few of you will wish to return. To these I now say-stay behind! You are better off here! And I cannot go on with my tale till I have asked whether there are any among you who would prefer the life of this quiet dale to that of the outer world, with its Power, its mountains, and its living dead."

HE made a pause, and for a breathing space none stirred. Then a maid of the company arose, sobbing; she cast her shawl over her face and said she would live and die in Alvrosdale; then she went forth from the Hall. With her went likewise the young man of her choice, and as the door of the Hall clanged to behind them, the rest sat the closer and gave ear to the voice of the old man.

"There are none now left alive," he said, "who remember Hal Hallstrom in his youth; but I give you my word that it was as lusty a youth as any of yours. I was light and gay and would roll the flavor of adventure under my tongue. In those days, before the year 4060 A. D., as was the

Kartindo Books (Kartindo.com)

reckoning, there, were legends of the lords of old, and how the Demon Power drove them through the skies and over the waters and under the earth. But they were the rusty legends of those who tell a tale without understanding its meaning. This very Hall of Assembly was held to be the home of the Demon Power, a place so accursed that none dare approach it. This Demon was believed to be the same who had so dealt with the Mountain of the South that it fell across the neck of our dale and cut it off from the world in long past ages. We know now that this is not true; but men thought otherwise then.

"In those days I heard also legends that came down from my fathers' fathers, how, when the Mountain of the South closed off the dale, the Anglesk sent men through the air to bring us this thing and that; but such tales were held foolish beyond words. Now, lo!-we ourselves fly through the air, though not as the Anglesk with the aid of the Demon Power.

"Also there were legends of the splendor of the villages of the Anglesk: how they piled stone on stone to make mountainous dwellings in which the night was bright as day by suns of their own contriving; how they quarreled and slew each other from afar with thunderbolts; how the voices of men long dead spoke to them from Machines, and the voices of men far away spoke to them through the clouds.

"Old wives' tales? But I was young, and youth must ever test the false and true by the touchstone of experience, even as you now go forth to do.... One who has reached my age seeks neither for truth nor beauty any more, but only for rest." Herewith, one of the elders touched the arm of the old man, who thereupon looked around and, as one who has been recalled to his narrative, went on.

Wanderlust

"ON a day in spring, then, as I was in charge of the flock close by the brink where Oster Dalalven plunges into the channel that carries it under the Mountain of the South, I was seized with a great longing to see these dwellings where men moved in light and music.

"Thereupon, so hasty was my mood, I slung my quiver over my shoulder without more ado, and with staff in hand set out for the Mountain of the South, making a wide circuit to the east to go around this very House of Power.

"In those days few in Alvrosdale and none outside could equal me as a cragsman. But I had need of all my skill, for, as I advanced, the edges of the Mountain of the South became ever more rugged, torn into heaps and pinnacles as sharp as daggers. All morning long I clambered among the rocky screes, not seldom tearing clothes or skin, and at noon made pause and ate, though sparingly, of the bread and cheese that I had brought for my lunch. Of water there was none, nor did I see any sign of trees or other life. The Mountain of the South is a vast wilderness of stone, hard and desolate, not mellowed with age like our summits of the Keel.

Kartindo Books (Kartindo.com)

"But still my heart was high, and after my midday meal I took to climbing again. My road grew worse; thrice I was near to death, as some ledge I was on ran out into sheerest precipice without room to turn back. The loneliness of the place weighed down upon my spirit also, for all that day I saw no living thing-I, who had always known the kindly dale of Alvros, where the cow-bells tinkle ever within hearing. And at night I made camp just below the edge of the line where the snows mantle the rugged pinnacles.

"In the morn, as I started on, I still saw the summit towering far above me, and now I dared not turn back, for fear of the rocks and avalanches. All day I tramped the snow. Toward afternoon I found a glacier that eased my labor somewhat; yet up it I must move with utmost caution, for there were great crevasses running down for miles into its heart, often so hidden that it was not until I thrust my stick down through the crust of snow that they became visible. That night I built myself a cairn of ice in the lee of a rock, and camped supperless and cold.

"I AWOKE so stiff that the third day of my ascent was like to be my last. A storm had come up and veiled the head of the mountain; I was weak with the chill, the wounds in my hands were nipped by the icy blast, and my hunger had become a terrible gnawing pain. The glacier petered out and I had to clamber among rocks again-rocks that were covered with a glare of ice.

"The wind shrieked about me among the rocks; the storm blotted out all knowledge of the sun, and I knew that if another night found me on that bleak summit, all nights and days would end for me. Yet I kept on! I came at last to a place where a wall of ice-covered rock rose sheer before me; to right and left there seemed no passage, and I halted, ready to lie down in blank despair. But as I stood still, I caught sight of a black shape amid the gray of the whirling snow, and a great golden eagle swept down on the wings of the wind past me, swung off suddenly to the left and, just at the limit of my sight, turned again over the rocky wall.

"I took it for an omen and followed down the wall to where the eagle had disappeared. Sure enough, there lay a narrow chimney through the rock, that might not otherwise have been seen. I leapt into it, stumbling and slipping on the loosened stones, but going upward; and a few minutes later I had reached the top of the wall, and with it the crest of the mountain!"

The old man paused, and in the hall one might see a stir of motion, as his hearers, stiffened by listening to his recital, changed their position. He-paused and looked around, as though loath to believe that he was not living again the brave days of his adventure. Then he began once more.

"It is unlikely that any, however expert cragsmen they may be, will follow my path; for we now have the wings and follow the raven, soaring over that perilous tower with never a break. But if, through courage, you should wish to attempt it, I warn you-do not venture! For I am convinced that only by the favor of the most high gods and by the omen of the golden eagle did I come through unscathed.

"When I had followed the eagle through the pass and stood indeed on the highest crest of the

Kartindo Books (Kartindo.com)

Mountain of the South, the storm cleared away as if by magic, and far beneath me I saw the Mountain spread out, and beyond the Mountain a smiling valley-like Alvrosdale, but broader and deeper. Through the heart of it trailed our own river-Oster Dalalven-after it had burst foaming from the rocks beneath the mountain. Beside it was a white ribbon of a road that ran off into the distance. Along the road I could see the habitations of men, gleaming in the afternoon sunlight, and forests that ran down almost to the houses and at times hid the road. I shouted for joy at the prospect and began the descent of the mountain; for in that moment I knew that the tales of a world of splendor were based in truth.

Kartindo Books (Kartindo.com)

Chapter II
: Beyond the Mountain

"HALF an hour later I shot a ptarmigan amid the snow and so tasted meat for the first time in three days. This was the greatest luck, for the descent was worse than the climb on the other side had been. For a day I floundered amid the drifts, and came at last to a place that dropped sheer for half a mile. There was no descent, so I had to turn back and try this way and that. Three days I spent thus, going down and coming back, climbing and descending, before I deviously reached the bottom. On the second day I tasted once more the kindness of the gods, for my foot touched a stone that touched another and suddenly set off a landslide that cleared my path down the worst of the steeps.

"At last I stood at the base of the mountain, a place by no means lacking in piled rocks, but with no more dizzy descents. For a time I lay on my face, prostrate, and clasped the fair grass with my bruised hands-grass that felt softer to them than after the longest winter! Then I arose and, with such strength as I had left, staggered to the brim of Oster Dalalven and plunged my face in the water; then by the brim of the stream I fell asleep, though the sun was still high in the heavens.

"I woke in the chill of dawn, with the memory of a sound ringing in the back of my head. As I started to my feet, I heard again the sound that had roused me-the baying of a dog- and in a moment it was answered by multiple voices, as when a pack of our Alvrosdale hounds course on the trail of a rabbit.

"Surely,' I thought, 'there must be men not far away in this dale, since there are men's dogs here,' and I climbed up onto a boss of rock the better to see my way and the dogs that had sounded. As I reached the crest of the stone, the hounds swept into view from the road not a hundred paces to my left, and came tearing along among the stones-dogs indeed, but such as I had never seen, strong and terrible of aspect, and not on the trail of a rabbit, but of a great antlered deer. In a moment they were past, but two of the later members of the pack paused when they came to where I had passed, sniffing and growling over the place where I had slept

" 'IF all the Anglesk are as great as their dogs, then theirs is indeed a mighty race,' I thought. The road itself was curious, all overgrown and the stones pushed apart by grass and weeds; and the dried grass of other summers lay among the fresh, as though it had been there for a long time. Yet I mused not overmuch on it, for the road led up under the Mountain of the South, and all men knew how that hill had risen between Alvrosdale and the world in a single night, breaking sheer across the road and all else.

"Perhaps a mile or two further along I saw houses clustered in a hamlet between road and river. Among them all there was no sign of life and while it might have been the earliness of the hour, I remarked it because of the other signs of desolation on that journey and my heart misgave me. And as I drew near I was more surprised than ever, for in all that village, which by the legends of

Kartindo Books (Kartindo.com)

the dale should have been a great and splendid place, there was neither sound of voice, bark of dog, nor sign of smoke in the chimneys. A fear came upon me, and I ran forward, weak as I was. But at the first house my fear was confirmed. The door hung all awry with rust marks at its side- the doorsill split and dug up by the frosts of winter, and the broken windows looking in on ruin and desolation.

"I hastened to the next house and the next, and so on through the village. Some were of stone and some of purest glass, but all alike were empty; it was a village of the dead, but with no sign of dead or living. Only at the end of the village did I hear the bleating of sheep and, going to the spot, came upon a flock-not well-kept, fat sheep such as we house in Alvrosdale, but thin and lank, and their coats filled with briars. At my approach they made off toward the forest. I bent my bow against them and slew a ewe, and taking of her meat went to one of the houses, thinking to cook the meat in that ruined town; but in no house that I entered was there so much as a fireplace-all were filled with Machines, now fallen to dust and rust, and other appliances whose use I did not understand; so I built my fire in the open, using dead branches from the trees.

"The food refreshed me much, and packing in my scrip as much more of it as I could conveniently carry, I followed the road onward. Further down I came upon another House of Power, so like this that the two might have been built by the same hand; and with fear strong within me I swung wide around it, yet had no need, for like all else in this dale, it was lifeless.

The Dead City

"IT is sad to me even now in retrospect to think of coming to that place after a journey of so much arduousness. For in all that land of the Anglesk I found no living man nor heard any voice save those of the wild dogs as they bayed now near, now far, For days I journeyed thus; many villages I passed, all well built and strong and beautiful, most of them made of shining glass, testifying to the glory of the Anglesk. All were filled with Machines of much marvel-and all were fallen to ruin and rust, befouled by beasts, streaked with the wet of rains and rent by tempests. At night I often lay in the cellars of these houses. By day I walked, killing now a sheep and now a hog, according to my need and as I came upon them. One day I came to a place where the houses grew thicker and the forest had retreated until the village was the greatest ever seen by the eye of man. Some of these houses were like those I had heard of in legends-mighty towers whose tops soared to the clouds, built all of stone and bronze so that the tooth of time had hardly touched them. But all were dead and deserted like the rest, with only birds to nest behind the broken windows, and swine to wander among the streets of that melancholy place.

"I wandered to and fro among the streets for close upon a day, and as twilight fell I made preparations to find a cellar for the night. But as I did this I saw among the myriad towers a single one that held a light in its window. A great, fierce hope sprung up in me that living men might be here, though mingled with it was the fear that it was only a trap of the Demon Power to lure me into his clutches. However, for what purpose had I come so far in such a melancholy land-but to adventure? So I made for this tall tower as rapidly as I might through all the tangled

Kartindo Books (Kartindo.com)

maze of streets.

"Night had come on before I reached it. I came upon it suddenly, swinging around the corner of another tower upon a square of forest land let into that village. A fox stirred in the underbrush as I crossed this square and for a moment a dark owl soared between me and the spring moon. The tower rose before me-a mountain of stone and glass, like the Mountain of the South in size but all dark and silent behind its windows, save some four or five near the base, and a whole floor high up, from which came the light I had seen.

"I drew near and saw a flight of steps that led up to a great bronze door. It would not yield to my push, nor was there any answer to my knocking. As it was already late, I looked for a place to spend the night so that I might attempt the adventure of the tower again when day should come.

"WHEN the sun gilded the towers of the great village, I rose to try again. As before, I found the bronze doors locked fast against me; but the building was of great extent as well as height, and I did not desist, thinking there might be some other way in. I had not looked far when I came upon another and smaller door, set level with the street. This I tried; it gave a little to my push and I set my shoulder against it. As I did so, door and lock burst, and I plunged in.

"I stood in a long hall, lit dimly by the tall and narrow windows at the side of the door I had entered. At either side there was a long row of doors. With my mind now made up to follow the venture through, I tried the first. It would not open; but the trick of its movement as I pushed it showed me that it was a sliding panel door, and, slipping it to one side, I stepped in. I found myself in a room no larger than a closet in my father's house in Alvrosdale, windowless as that same closet, and very dark. The door had slid into place behind me. I groped for it, and it is in my mind that I must have touched some Machine within the wall of the room, for forthwith there rose a humming sound, and when I put my hand out again, it touched a wall in rapid motion. The whole room was moving! . . . My friends, you cannot understand the terror of that moment; for I felt that I was in the very grip of the Demon Power. Though Power is an old and feeble demon now, in those days he was strong and malignant."

The old man paused and from the hand of one of the elders took a fragrant draught of mead; and when he paused, a low sigh of interest and excitement ran around the hall, for all those folk had been brought up to fear Power and Machines as the most deadly of things.

"In real life men do not faint or go mad with terror, when in such situations," said the old man, beginning again. "They seek for some means of escape. But even as I sought to escape from that moving room, there came a louder buzz and it stopped as suddenly as it had moved. A shaft of light filtered in at the top and showed me that it had stopped before a door. I flung it open-anything was better than that small moving closet. I stood in a long hall with sunlight streaming through the glass walls and reflecting back in dazzling radiance from row on row of great ingots of silver.

Kartindo Books (Kartindo.com)

" SO much wealth neither I nor anyone in this dale has ever seen. Yet there was something curious about those ingots, when I looked at them a second time, for each one was laid on a table by itself, and each seemed rather a close winding of many wires than a solid piece of that precious metal. Dumb with astonishment at the sight, I stood for a moment, and then approached one of them, thinking that they might be a dream wrought for my undoing by the Demon Power. I noted that the form of the silver winding had, from a little distance, a certain likeness to that of a man, from one side of which many of the wires were collected and twisted through holes in a slab of stone on which the form lay.

"The likeness to the form of a man increased as I approached, and when I came and stood directly over it, I saw that it was indeed a man, but a dead one-all swathed and wound in silver wires which, as they drew near his body, drew into finer and finer wires till right over the skin they were spread out like silver spider webs, half-concealing his features. The dead man had a grave and reverend aspect, like a priest of the gods; no hair grew on his head nor beard on his face, for even here the silver wires lay over him.

"All this I took in at a glance, and in the same moment the thought came over me that each of these piles of silver was a man, dead like the first. I stepped back in horror. As I did so, my hand touched the tangle of silver wires from one of the dead, and all up my hand and arm ran a tingling jar! At the same moment the dead man before me stirred ever so slightly. With the horror of that moment my tongue was loosed; I shrieked and fled. Around and around the room I ran, like a rat trapped in a cage. At last I reached a door and flung it open, not on another narrow room, but on a stair, and up this I fled without taking account of direction . . .

"You will understand that, although the place is of, ill omen and hence forbidden for our folk to approach, it is in no wise deadly; but I did not know this. I thought that these living dead were under the shadow of the Demon Power and that the jar I had received was a warning not to disturb their sleep, lest I become like them . . . But the staircase up which I fled gave on another hall, filled, like the first, with row upon row of those living corpses, lapped in silver. As in the hall below, the walls were all of glass; and the coiled silver cables, where the thin wires of this most precious metal united, were twisted from the sides of the sleepers and passed through holes in the slabs.

"Yet all this I hardly noted, for I fled again, and so to another hall, and another, and yet another, up and down the stairs seeking only to leave that accursed place. I do not know how long I ranged thus up and down. I only know that at last, stumbling downward, I came to a door that led upon a long passage. Down it I went, though it was narrow, and at one side a Machine hung over the edge of the passage to grip the passer-by the instant the Demon Power should will it.

Kartindo Books (Kartindo.com)

Chapter III

: The Man with the Metal Mask

"AT the end the passage divided in two. Not knowing which turn would lead me from the building, I chose the right, but had hardly gone twenty paces when before me I saw the low flare of a light and heard a mighty clanking. Surely, I thought, this is the very abode of the Demon Power himself, and I turned back with a new fright to add to the old.

"This time I took the other branch. As I went down it, I again saw a light ahead-but to what purpose would it be to turn back? Moreover I had now somewhat gained control of myself, and so, saying-'A man who is fated to die will surely die, whereas a man fated to live shall walk through perils,'-I strode on. And lo! the shaft of light came from a room, and near the door of the room sat a man, a veritable living man in a chair with a board before him, on which he moved small carved figures. As I entered, he turned to me a face that was not a face, but a metal mask, and said some words to me in a tongue which I did not understand. Overcome with fatigue, I fell at his feet...."

Again the old man paused and drank a draught of mead, then seated himself for a brief space, while in the Hall arose a whirr of voices that were stilled again when he rose once more.

"When I awoke I was lying on the floor of the room where I found the man with the metal face, and it seemed that he looked upon me with kindness. In his hand he held vessels, which he extended to me, making signs that I should eat and drink, and though the food was strange I ate and was refreshed. I spoke to him quickly, asking what this city of the living dead was, and where were the people of so glorious a town and what had become of the Anglesk, but he only shook his head and sat down again to his board, which was marked out in squares of alternate black and white. Then, taking one of the carved figures from the board, he held it up to me, and said-'Rook.' I examined it-it was in the likeness of a tower of stone-but it conveyed no meaning whatever to me, so I banded it back with a smile for his courtesy. Therewith the man with the metal face sighed deeply and motioned me to a seat beside him, while he went on moving the carved figures here and there, making notes on a piece of paper he held in his hand the while.

"I looked about; the room was long rather than wide, and along one wall of it ran a great board, from which loops of wire jutted, entering into little holes. Presently a red light shone from the board and the man with the metal face rose, and with slow and halting steps, like one of great age, went to the board and transferred one of the loops from one hole to another; then returned to his table.

"FOR a long time I waited, watching the man with the metal face. He said no more-nor did I. But after a time he arose and, motioning that I should follow him, led me through the other end of the room. There he showed me a bed; It was narrow and low, and covered not with blankets but with a single web of a weave marvelously fine and softer to the fingers than anything I had ever

Kartindo Books (Kartindo.com)

touched. The room was filled with a pleasant fragrance like that of the woods in spring, though there was no window and we were far from the trees.

"He signed that I should lay myself on the bed, and when I had done so he brought forth from some corner a Machine like a cap, fitting close to the head, with special parts to cover the ears, and this he placed on my head. I started back in fright at it, for I thought it some new device to trap me deeper into the lures of the Demon Power. But the man with the metal face spoke kindly, and placed the cap on his own head to show that no harm was intended.

"With that I lay down on the bed and slept, and knew no more, though my sleep was shot with dreams in which the living dead rose and spoke to me in the tongue of the Anglesk, and told me of frightful things.... To you, my friends, it will seem strange that men should speak in another tongue than ours. Yet so it was in the days of the Anglesk, that different men in different dales had different words for the same thing and could no more understand one another than we could understand the babbling of a child or the bark of a fox.

"In the morning I awoke fresh and rested after my sleep. The man with the metal face was bending over me, and as I sat up in the first wild surprise at finding myself in this so unfamiliar place, he bent over and detached the Machine I had been wearing through the night.

"Do you play chess?' he asked; not in our own words, but in the tongue of the Anglesk of old; and, wonder of all wonders, I understood him.

"What?' I cried in astonishment. 'How is it that I now understand what you say, though it is in a different way from our own speech?'

"Oh, that is the radio helmet,' he replied, treating the matter as one of no import. 'But tell me, do you play chess?' His speech was thick and slow, as though passed through lips unable to properly form the words.

"Chess?' I answered. 'I don't know the name. Is it a game of the Anglesk?'

"The man with the metal face sighed deeply and half to himself said: 'And for twenty years I have been bringing my Sayers gambit to absolute perfection-my legacy to the world.' Of this I understood nothing, but he said aloud: 'Yes, I am one of the Anglesk, as you call them, though our name is the English. I am the last.' And again the man with the metal face sighed.

"Questions rushed to my lips. 'Then what does all this mean?' I asked. 'Who built this glorious village and these shining towers with the spider-like bridges from one to another, and where are those who should live in them? And who are the living dead that sleep above?"

"'They are the English,' said the man with the metal face, 'all that are left of them. Now let us eat and I will explain it to you; but first you shall tell me how you came here, ignorant of Machines

Kartindo Books (Kartindo.com)

and civilization, and yet with a white skin.'

Tale of the Machine Man

"I FELL in with his humor and with him partook of his curious foods; then sat in the room of the board and table, where ever and again the red light flashed and the man with the metal face ceased his talking and changed a loop of silver wire from one hole to another. I told him of Alvrosdale and of our life there; how we hunted and tilled the ground and tended our flocks; and of the Mountain of the South and how I had climbed over it with the aid of the most high gods. It was a tale of which he did not weary. He plied me with meat and drink, and learned what I knew. Then he told me his tale in turn, which I will rehearse to you."

At this saying the old man paused again, and again drank from the mead-horn. And as he began the tale of the man with the metal face, the hall was hushed to hear him.

"Know, man of Alvrosdale (the man with the metal face told me) that I am of an age compared to which you are but a babe in arms, for I count beyond a hundred summers, and so does the least of those sleepers above. Much have I seen and heard and read, and of one thing I am sure-that you are a part of a race which for thousands of summers has been shut away from the progress of civilization. You have no business in this dying world today, and when you have heard how it is with us, you had best go back over your mountain, there to stay. Or perhaps you will gather companions, and out of your dale come to people a new world.

"Know that long centuries ago-about the year 1950 A. D.-the world held countless hundreds of millions of people. There were men whose skins were black, and men with yellow skins and even with red skins; but they were mostly barbarians, and hence I was surprised at your own arrival, for I thought all the men with white skins had died long ago. The men with white skins were, in truth, the greatest of peoples; they had spread out and conquered all the rest of the world, so that the black and yellow and red men toiled for them. Now of all the white men, the greatest were the English; they moved fastest and strongest across the face of the earth; they founded colonies, and the colonies themselves grew to be greater than other nations.

"In elder ages men quarreled, this group and that, and fought destructive wars in which thousands were slain by the use of guns, which hurled great pieces of steel that rent and tore asunder all that stood in their path. But among the English and the colonies of the English were many great scientists. These scientists designed Machines called Radio, fashioned so cunningly that a man had but to speak in them to he heard afar by many men in other lands. Now in the days of which I speak, the English spoke into their Radio and their tongue spread across the whole world. Then the quarrelling of nations ceased, for there is no quarrel that may not be settled by simple words when men may speak these words understanding to one another.

"THAT was long after the Mountain of the South had risen to shut off your dale. The people of your dale may have heard of the wonders of our civilization, though it is not likely. We had

Kartindo Books (Kartindo.com)

Machine's that flew through the air and bore many passengers across the oceans; Machines that grew crops for us, tending them carefully and driving away the insects; Machines that transformed these crops into food without the intervention of hands. We built great cities, of which this is one of the least; cities of majestic buildings, all of glass, in which men lived lives of ease and pleasure. Pleasure! That was the cause of the whole tragedy of our world. We did not know that the pursuit of pleasure alone, which had been our guide, was to be our ruin.

"Can you Imagine, barbarian of Alvrosdale, what it is to be free from the necessity of earning your bread? You cannot-for you belong to another age and another race. But the English all over the world, and the men of other races who had become English, now had nothing to do. The sources of Power were so inexhaustible, and the amount of work necessary to make them available so slight, that half an hour's labor a day sufficed to earn a man his living. And the Machines continued to grow ever more complex and more ingenious.

"Adventure, which is the pastime of many men, disappeared, when war became obsolete. For some people, art filled the vacant hours. But as the scientists grew in knowledge, the Machines they made executed the arts better than the artists themselves. Music was the first of the arts to disappear. First there were Machines that recorded the performances of great musicians and reproduced them to all hearers at any time. Then came Machines that gave these reproductions to vast audiences, and others that showed the audiences such lifelike pictures of the musicians that they seemed to be present in person. And finally Machines were invented that altogether eliminated the musician, striking the correct tones and shades of tones with scientific accuracy.

"The picture Machines, that brought an end to music, were the beginning of the end of the art of the theatre-you hardly know what a theatre is? It is, or was, a place where people acted stories. With the going of theatres, too, there were fewer and fewer artists, and finally we had only mere puppets. Sculpture, which was a kind of carving, was the next art to cease. The scientists made Machines that felt gently over living persons and carved their likenesses out of enduring stone or wood.

Kartindo Books (Kartindo.com)

Chapter IV
: Adventure is Dead

"BUT why tell you more? You have heard enough to understand that art, the last refuge of men of leisure, was destroyed by the very Machines that gave man the leisure to enjoy art.... So it was with everything. Adventure of all kinds died. The last depths in the earth were plumbed, the last mountains were climbed or flown over by the might of the Machines. Men even made Machines to travel to the other planets that circle around the sun; they went to them, found them all inhospitably hot, cold or airless.

"And even here the Machines did away with all those occupations which provide adventure; for adventure is always the outcome of some lawless act, and the scientists had eliminated lawlessness by eliminating criminals soon after the coming of universal peace. Machines tested every child psychologically and supplied the proper remedies to make him a good citizen. . . .

"You must picture, my barbarian friend, a world in which Machines had deprived men not only of labor, but of amusement, of adventure, of excitement-in short, of everything that makes life worth while. Oh they were terrible days of boredom! What was left? Only the frantic pursuit of artificial pleasures. And men did pursue pleasure to a degree which seems fantastic to even me. Men became connoisseurs of odors, of clothes; I, even I, have spent a month's income on a new perfume, and a thousand dollars for a single piece of cloth of original design. . . . But even here the Machines followed us, doing things better than we. We had nothing but leisure-endless, meaningless leisure.

"THEN the institution of Adventure Insurance arose. It began with a Japanese named Hatsu Yotosaki, who was hired to furnish new amusement-'thrills' they called it- to a party of rich Australians who had gone on an extended air voyage over Antarctica. This Jap conceived the idea of letting each member of the party know, indirectly, that some other one of the party was a criminal lunatic who was scheming to murder him. Long before their six months' cruise was up, they were all eyeing each other with suspicion and fright, prowling about the corridors of the airship at night and doing all the things men do under the influence of fear. Three of them were even killed by mistake.

"When they got back to Melbourne, Yotosaki told the survivors the story of how he had manufactured their fear and fright. Instead of jailing him for murder, they hailed him as a deliverer, the founder of a new idea. The idea was taken up with enthusiasm, and everywhere men were hired by others to involve them in wild and impossible, often bloody, adventures.

"But even here the scientists tried to intervene with their Machines. Why, they argued, go to all this trouble and expense to provide adventures for oneself, when one could obtain them second-hand by attending the mechanized theatres? The answer of the public was that the second hand adventures of the theater were insipid, being without the element of personal contact; they

Kartindo Books (Kartindo.com)

gave the spectator none of the personal thrill that is part of a real adventure. This led to the formation of great companies to furnish adventures to people.

"Now the governments of the world grew worried, for with the coming of universal freedom from labor, pleasure and its pursuit had become the main concern of government. They accordingly set the scientists to work to find an antidote to the adventure companies, which had succeeded in eluding government control . . . The result is what you see! This building and these people that you call the living dead.

"It did not come all at once, young man. You see only the finished product. At first the scientists sought only to make their mechanized theaters more perfect. They had already perfected sound and motion in the early ages; to this was now added a device that added the sense of smell; if the pictured story was laid in a woodland the scent of piny branches swept through the audience, and if at sea, there was the tang of the salt spray.

"But the people tired of these shows; they came and were amused for once, but never came again. The scientists then produced the sensations of heat and cold-people went to winter pictures wrapped in furs as though for a trip to the arctic regions; vast artificial winds stormed through the theaters to the tune of the swaying boughs in the pictures; clouds of smoke and tongues of veritable burning flame were rolled out over the audience; and at last devices were introduced which gave the sitters gentle electrical shocks at emotional moments in the performances.

"And now came the great discovery. It happened that a man had had his hand cut off in an accident. It had been the custom previously to provide such unfortunates with artificial limbs of marvelous ingenuity and dexterity. Now the man's surgeon, whose name was Brightman, suggested a metal hand which should be controlled by silver wires; and that the ends of the silver wires should be drawn out exceedingly fine, and attached to the nerves controlling the motions of the fingers. The nerves of the body are themselves like wires; they carry the messages of the brain to the muscles and of the muscles back to the brain. What Brightman was proposing was that the brain should deliver its message to the artificial metal nerves, thus causing the metal hand to move as a live hand would. It was his theory that all nervous impulses are delivered by electrical means, and if this was true the process would work.

"THE theory was not new, nor the idea; but previously there had been lacking any means to connect the metal wires to the nerves. This time it was done by the process discovered for building up human protoplasm; the connection between the silver wire and the nerve was made; it was placed in an electrical bath and given an atomic bombardment; and behold! the connecting end of the silver wire became itself a nerve wire of the same material as the rest of the nerve!

"Thus the plan worked-at first not well nor rapidly, but it worked. And as it was tried in succeeding cases, it worked better and better until a perfect artificial hand could be produced that was as good as a new one. . . . The next step came when the plan was applied to a man who had

Kartindo Books (Kartindo.com)

hopelessly lost his sight. Back of each eye is one of these nerves, which carries the message of what you see to the brain. For this man they made a new pair of eyes, fitted with machines called photo-sensitive cells, such as those I bear on my own face. In them is a marvel-metal called potassium, which, when light falls upon it, changes in resistance to an electrical current. Thus, for every speck of light there was a change in the electrical current that ran through the Machine, and the change was communicated to one of a net of wires, which in turn communicated it to the nerve of the eye. Then the man, though without eyes, could see!

"In time, this grew to be the common treatment for those who had lost their eyes, just as mechanical hands and feet replaced those members. And to one of our scientists (Professor Bruce) there came a new idea: If a man could by these means see what really happened, why should he not see also things that have never occurred? ... Do you understand?

"After a long experimentation Bruce found that if the photo-sensitive cell of a blind man were removed, and the silver wires that led to his optic nerve were attached to other wires, electrical currents could be sent down these other wires that would make him see things that were not actually there at all.

"All this was before the adventure associations sprang up. At the time these associations came into being, the scientists had achieved so high a state of perfection with the device of providing blind persons with sights they did not actually see, that the result was, the blind could be made to see almost anything, even a whole series of nonexistent events.

Kartindo Books (Kartindo.com)

Chapter V
: A Drastic Experiment

"THIS was the situation when the growth of the adventure associations began to threaten the basis of organized government. For the adventure associations promoted disorder among those very elements of the people who should most desire security. The head of a great food company, for example, was involved in an adventure. In the course of it he was attacked by several men who struck at him with clubs. One of them struck a trifle too hard; the food company head was killed, and his company suffered from it.

"In an evil hour, some scientist suggested to the New Zealand government that the people should be offered plays they could witness through their optic nerves, and thus experience them as actual. This would be a substitute for the adventures of the associations. The government accepted the suggestion. It would necessitate removing the eyes of the subjects, and providing them with photo-sensitive cells. A man who trusts his whole life to an adventure association would certainly be willing to submit to the slight inconvenience of seeing through a mask instead of through his eyes for the rest of his life.

"At first there was no great rush on the part of the people to accept the operation. A few did so, and gave glowing accounts of the results; but to submit to an operation whose results would be permanent for the sake of a few hours or even days of visual pleasure did not appeal to the majority. But it was at once apparent that if electrical impulses could be arranged so that the subject would see things that were not in existence, others could be similarly arranged to reach the senses of smell, and even of feeling, taste or what you will. Like the original operation on the eyes, the process of development was slow; it was over a hundred years from the time when the New Zealand government first offered its citizens operations on the eyes to the date when the completed Adventure Machines such as you have seen were produced in all their complexity. The type of electrical impulse to produce the desired sensation on every nerve had first to be found, then applied, and finally woven into a complex record to be placed in a Machine with other records to provide the Machine Adventurer with a complete series of sensations.

"THE final process was that the subject was operated upon by skilled surgeons. Every nerve in the body was laid bare, one after another; eyes, ears, nerves of feeling and taste, nerves of motion. To each was attached the tiny silver wire, and each was given the atomic treatment, then led down with the others to form a cable. During the first part of the operation the subject was placed under anaesthesia, but at the end, until his record was connected up, he experienced no sensations at all; he merely existed in an inert state, devoid of animation or feeling.

"As one set of nerves after another yielded its secrets to the scientists, the government Adventure Machines began to grow popular. They had enormous advantages over the adventure associations. The associations offered personal adventure that was often deadly; the Government Machines were absolutely safe. The adventure associations were costly; the Government device

Kartindo Books (Kartindo.com)

cost nothing, for when the subject submitted to the operation he was regarded by the courts as legally dead and his property passed to the Government. The adventure associations could offer only violent, physical adventures; the Government method could give the adventurer whatever he wanted. They could enable him to get the most out of life in whatever way he wished, for records of every sort were prepared, suited to the psychology of the individual.

"Thus if the operator wished to make the Adventurer feel that he was hunting, the record of a hunting adventure was placed in the Machine, and the cable leading from the adventurer's nerves was connected to it. The nerves of the adventurer's foot would assure him that he trod the mould of the forest; the nerves of his eyes would bring him a vision of the dim vista of trunks and a wild animal bounding through them; the nerves of his hands and arms would tell him he was making the correct motions to take aim and bring the animal down; and through the nerves of his ears, the Machine Adventurer would hear the dying scream of the beast he had slaughtered.

"THESE records are of an immense complexity; all the lower stories of this building are filled with them. It would not have done to make them too simple, for in that case the Machine Adventurer would have done better to have joined one of the associations. As it was, the Machine Adventurer chose his general type of adventure; his psychological charts, made when he was young, showed the type of mind he possessed, and what his reactions would be in certain cases. With the charts and his choice before them, the Government operators would lay out a course of adventures for him, and after the operation, he would pass through them in succession. There was a large number of adventures to choose from. Did he, for instance, wish to know what the distant planets looked like? In that case he would be given an adventure in which he was the head of an expedition. Under the spell of the Machine he gathered men and materials; with his own hands he worked on a space ship; he saw friends and companions about him, and all his senses reeled to the shock as his ship sprang away from the earth. He even felt that he ate and drank during the trip, for the nerves of taste and digestion were connected up as well as the others. At last he saw the new planet he was to visit swimming in the skies, larger and larger, as his ship approached it.

"You see the advantages? Men could achieve anything by this means; they could have the experience of accomplishing not only everything possible in actual life, but a great many things that actual life never holds even for the most fortunate. They could, if they were of the proper type, return to the cave-man period of existence and bounce over the hummocky moss in pursuit of the hairy rhinoceros, or float as disembodied spirits down endless corridors of an artificial Nirvana.

"IN fact, there was but one thing the Machine Adventurer could not do: he could not return to the world. For the operations, once undergone, were practically irreversible. They involved, as I have said, laying bare every nerve of the body and by atomic bombardment making it an integral part of the silver wire that carried the false messages of sensation to it. To reverse the operation would naturally leave the returned Machine Adventurer deaf, dumb, blind and helpless, a mere living jelly. But nobody wished to return. The Adventure Houses, like this one, contained a vast

Kartindo Books (Kartindo.com)

store of records; the adventurers themselves were practically immortal and merely passed the rest of their days in a series of pleasing and thrilling experiences that always ended happily. Some of the more complex adventures, like those in which the subjects found themselves in the roles of world conquerors, lasted over a period of years, and as soon as one was ended, the operators in the offices of the Adventure Houses switched the subject onto a new adventure.

"People readily abandoned the outside world in which everything was rapidly becoming dead. The adventure associations died as quickly as they had been born. After all, the majority of men and nearly all women soon tired of the crude excitements these adventure associations provided. In a short time whole groups of people undertook Machine Adventures; and the world's population, which had been rising ever since the apes first descended from their trees, began to fall.

"At this point the very scientists who had developed the Machines began to become alarmed at the great rush of people to use them. They advised the destruction of the machines and the substitution of some other method of providing thrills and adventures. But the governments of the world, successful and peaceful and secure as no governments had ever been before, turned their backs on the scientists and built more and greater Adventure Houses. The scientists attempted to appeal to the people over the heads of the governments. The people laughed at them; and the governments paid no attention until one group of Oriental scientists, more devoted or less prudent than the rest, destroyed the great Adventure House at Chien-po by concentrating destructive rays upon it. This roused the governments to action; they rounded up all the disagreeing scientists and instead of executing them, forcibly operated upon them and placed them in Adventure Houses.

"The battle was a losing one on the side of the scientists from the start. One after another they grew old and abandoned the hopeless struggle, preferring themselves to enter the Adventure House and have a couch of ease and pleasant experiences.

"I cannot, I am afraid, picture for you the universal decay of every kind of life save that furnished by the Adventure Machines. Adventure Machines for even the little children were produced. . . . After while it became difficult to find operators for the Machines; cities and towns were practically depopulated. Even the black barbarians succumbed, for they had their Adventure Machines as the white men had theirs. In the Machines, be he never so fond of the pleasures of life, every man found every pleasure enhanced to the nth degree. The glutton, the drunkard, the man mad over women found here his own special paradise. Everything else became useless . . ."

Kartindo Books (Kartindo.com)

"WITH these words," continued Hal Halstrom, looking over the hall, "the voice of the man with the metal face trailed off and he sat babbling in his chair like one grown mad. So I even let him babble on, while I sat in silence. And after a time he rose and prepared meat for us and we did eat.

"But still some doubts and questions troubled my mind, how such things could be; and I asked him: 'How came it that you escaped to tell this tale?'

"'I did not escape,' he said, touching the metal mask that covered all his face. 'Don't you see this? It is the badge of my own servitude to the Machines. I, no less than the rest, underwent the operation. And oh, the delight of it! For I was born by the shore of the sea, and in my adventure I swam forever among the green depths and saw strange monsters. I would willingly have been left there. But a day came when the last of the operators of this Adventure House died, and the three surgeons, who were all that were left, took me from the Machine and brought me back to this cruel world, for I was in those days an engineer and they needed me to operate the Machine. For my eyes they gave me these Machines, for my ears other Machines, and the tips of my hands and feet-all, all, I am a Machine! The mark of the Machine is on me. . . .

"He cried these last words so wildly that I was fearful he might again fall into his insensate babbling. So I broke in upon him. 'But these Adventurers,' I asked, 'how do they eat?'

"His lip curled with scorn of my ignorance. 'In truth,' he said, 'you are a barbarian of the early ages that do not know of the D'Arsonval diathermic method. Know then, that among the silver wires on each Adventurer's leg is clamped the end of an electric circuit, and at such times as meals are necessary, they are given electric meals of low and high frequency currents. I tell you because you ask, not because you will understand."

"Ah,' I said, for in truth I did not understand. 'And what is your work here?'

"'I change the adventures and see that the machinery does not break down.'

"But there are thousands of the living dead above. Do you change all the adventures as they run through them?'

The man with the metal face hesitated and stammered as one in embarrassment "I am supposed to," he said finally, "but I am all alone now. It is too much. These few"-he waved his hand at the board on the wall, "were friends of mine once, and their adventures I change."

"But what makes the Machines run?" I asked, seeing that he was cast down and wishing to draw him from his thoughts.

Kartindo Books (Kartindo.com)

"Power," said he. And then I shuddered, for I knew in good truth that I was in the very lair of that Demon.

"But where does Power come from, and who is he?" I asked, as boldly as I might.

For answer he took me by the hand and led me out of the room and down a. dizzy flight of iron stairs-down-down-to the very bowels of the earth. Finally he stopped and pointed. I saw a long shaft with a ruddy glow far at the base, and as I leaned over the iron rail a pebble that had somehow caught in my pocket tinkled from it against the rail and fell downward. I never heard it strike.

"There is the source of Power!" cried the man with the metal face. "The earth's central heat-for this world is fiery-hot at its core, and our scientists learned long ago how to tap it. I doubt me not that the first tapping was one reason why the mountain rose against your dale."

"WITH that we fell into conversation on this thing and that, and I stayed with him for many days.

"In the end I was fain to return to my own place, but knew not how to surmount the Mountain of the South again, so I begged the man with the metal face to help me out of the wisdom of the Anglesk.

"He thought on it for a time and said that he would help me, but when he would show me how to escape over the mountain by means of Power, I refused. So he thought out another plan, and offered to show me how to build these wings we now use, on condition that I do a certain thing for him-namely, take him with me so that he might look again upon the faces of living men and women, and hear them talk. I agreed to this and thereupon we left the living dead to repeat eternally their empty adventures.

"The man with the metal face was stricken by the brilliance of the day when outside, and not a little overcome at the appearance of those mighty towers. Yet the thought of meeting living people sustained him and he showed me the trick of these wings, calling them gilders, and training me in their use until I could fly with them, both fast and far, soaring down the currents of the wind like a bird. Thereupon we set out for the Mountain of the South and for Alvrosdale.

BUT ere we reached the place, the man with the metal face sickened and died; for we had exhausted such of his food as he brought with him from the tower, and the flesh of sheep and swine was over-rough fare for him, So perished the last of the Anglesk, and on his death he gave me this Machine with a voice, which he called an 'alarum clock,' to be a perpetual memento of the terror of Machines and the folly of the Anglesk.

"The man with the metal face I buried by a pile of stones, then buckled my wings to my back and soared away.
Kartindo Books (Kartindo.com)

"But when I returned to Alvrosdale bearing on my back the wings that were the proof of my tale, there was great hurry and bustle, and many would have taken the eagles' causeway outward as I had taken it inward, for in those days the dale was so crowded with folk that many could not have good fortune. Nevertheless the land would lie fallow if all went, or even a great part, and some must remain behind to care for those who returned broken in spirit or in body. Therefore this ceremony and the examinations through which you have passed were instituted. Each year the dale chooses of its best and boldest, and to them is told the tale you have heard before they start on the long journey. Now I leave you-and good luck attend your flight; but bear in mind that the villages and Machines of the Anglesk are accursed and belong to the living dead until their towers shall topple to the ground. Farewell."

With these words the old man sat down as one exhausted with long speech and with the memory of the trials and terrors of the past.

The dawn was streaking palely along the eastern windows of the Hall of Assembly, as the hearers of the tale arose and made their way gravely to the door.

In the doorway each was met by one who gave him a scrip of food, a pair of skis and a set of wings, and one after another they spun down the snowy hill, away from the Hall, to gather speed and finally to soar aloft in the clear wintry dawn, over the Mountain of the South, out into the dead world, with their cargo of new hopes and fears and aspirations.

THE END

Kartindo Books (Kartindo.com)

www.ingramcontent.com/pod-product-compliance
Lightning Source LLC
Chambersburg PA
CBHW070944290526
45795CB00003B/1137